Victorious Living

For New Christians

Fred Kinzie
Robert Henson
Wayne Mitchell

Victorious Living for New Christians

by Fred Kinzie, Robert Henson, and Wayne Mitchell

ISBN 1-56722-049-5

©1980 Word Aflame Press
Hazelwood, MO 63042-2299
Printing History: 1981, 1987, 1988, 1990, 1991, 1993, 1995, 1996, revised 1998

All Scripture quotations in this book are from the King James Version of the Bible unless otherwise identified.

All rights reserved. No portion of this publication may be reproduced, stored in an electronic system, or transmitted in any form or by any means, electronic, mechanical, photocopy, recording, or otherwise, without the prior permission of Word Aflame Press. Brief quotations may be used in literary reviews.

Printed in United States of America.

Printed by

Contents

Foreword 4

Introduction
   Welcome to a Brand-new Life 5

CHAPTER 1   What Has Really Happened to Me! 6

CHAPTER 2   Learning to Walk 11

CHAPTER 3   Encountering Conflict from Satan 18

CHAPTER 4   Your Church and You 26

CHAPTER 5   The World and You 32

CHAPTER 6   Your Home and You 43

Foreword

This book rises out of a long-standing need. For years our pastors have wished that they could present to a new convert under one cover inspirational instructions relative to his various Christian responsibilities. On a local level, some very fine booklets have been produced by some of our pastors. The success of their material has all the more pointed up the need for helpful publications being offered on a general basis.

The General Home Missions Division made contact with three of our very aggressive and successful pastors, with a request that they produce material for such a book. You will see that the experience and maturity of these men have shown strongly through these pages.

This is not an attempt to answer all questions. Neither is it an attempt to exhaust every subject. While this book avoids bulk and heavy theology, it does offer to a newborn child of God a concise glimpse of the responsible, worthwhile, and happy life that awaits him in the church of the living God.

I am sure that you will offer your sincere thanks along with ours to Brothers Fred Kinzie, Robert Henson, and Wayne Mitchell.

J. T. Pugh

Introduction
Welcome to a Brand-New Life

You are a very fortunate individual indeed. You have just begun an entirely new existence. You have started the journey of all journeys. The worldwide family of God welcomes you aboard on the journey that leads from earth to eternal glory. This brand-new life is a bold and exciting adventure, a life that you have never before experienced. The words of Joshua 3:4 are most appropriate: "Ye have not passed this way heretofore."

The fresh life will open to you a whole new world of experiences that are thrilling and exciting. Your newfound joys will completely overshadow the temporary afflictions, persecutions, difficulties, and setbacks that do occur along the way in one's spiritual walk. The stalwart apostle Paul said, "For which cause we faint not; but though our outward man perish, yet the inward man is renewed day by day. For our light affliction, which is but for a moment, worketh for us a far more exceeding and eternal weight of glory; while we look not at the things which are seen, but at the things which are not seen: for the things which are seen are temporal; but the things which are not seen are eternal" (II Corinthians 4:16-18).

Yes, difficulties and problems are to be expected in this brand-new life. However, the newfound hope and joy more than make it worthwhile. We also have the sweet assurance from the Scripture, "There hath no temptation taken you but such as is common to man: but God is faithful, who will not suffer you to be tempted above that ye are able; but will with the temptation also make a way to escape, that ye may be able to bear it" (I Corinthians 10:13).

Eternal life and the joy of companionship with Jesus—there is nothing greater. Welcome to a brand-new life!

CHAPTER 1

What Has Really Happened to Me!

You have been born into an abundant life! It is a life that is exciting, fresh, and truly alive. Everything about it glistens like raindrops that fall while the sun is shining. The first gentle breezes of your experience carry the fleeting fragrance of roses. It is indeed a great life and experience, but let us pause for a moment and examine what has really happened to you.

The modern thinking of our generation is that it makes little difference what people believe or which church they attend. But Scripture plainly declares that there is only one gospel that brings salvation to humanity. "But though we, or an angel from heaven, preach any other gospel unto you than that which we have preached unto you, let him be accursed" (Galatians 1:8). Our Lord Himself taught this fact. "Jesus saith unto him, I am the way, the truth, and the life: no man cometh unto the Father, but by me" (John 14:6).

The apostle Paul strongly affirmed that there is but one church and one faith. "There is one body, and one Spirit, even as ye are called in one hope of your calling; one Lord, one faith, one baptism" (Ephesians 4:4-5). Jesus spoke distinctly on the subject: "And I say also unto thee, That thou art Peter, and upon this rock I will build my church; and the gates of hell shall not prevail against it" (Matthew 16:18). We should note that in all of these scriptural references, there is never a mention made to two churches, or three gospels, or four truths, or five ways; but always the terms are singular: one church, one plan, one gospel, one way, one truth.

Conviction of Sins

Truth that we have never heard about does us very little good. For the work of proclaiming truth, God chose the ministry. A preacher's duty is to declare the truth to lost humanity. "How then shall they call on him in whom they have not believed? and how shall they believe in him of whom they have not heard? and how shall they hear without a preacher?" (Romans 10:14). "For after that in the wisdom of God the world by wisdom knew not God, it pleased God by the foolishness of preaching to save them that believe" (I Corinthians 1:21).

It is most evident from these verses of Scripture the importance that God places on the preacher. Hope for salvation begins when a God-called minister plants the truth of the Scriptures in the heart and mind of a hearer. You are privileged and fortunate to have had a preacher declare to you the truth. This exciting new life that you have just begun actually had its beginning at the moment when the truth captured your heart.

The preaching of the Scriptures and the declaration of the holiness of God produce conviction in the heart of the sinner. Sinful and proud flesh cannot stand unbowed and unbroken in the presence of a holy God. His holiness reveals our sinfulness and filthiness. This produces strong condemnation in one's life and drives him to his knees if he is really hungry for God.

Conviction is what moved you to take your first steps toward God.

Repentance of Sins

The first thing a sinner must do in order to find God is to repent. Repentance is a confessing and forsaking of sins along with a sincere cry for mercy and forgiveness. It is a turning around. It is resetting one's direction in life. Jesus taught us the absolute necessity of repentance. "I tell you, Nay: but, except ye repent, ye shall all likewise perish" (Luke 13:3). In Acts 2 the apostle Peter's first response to those who inquired concerning salvation was, "Repent." Repentance was your first substantial step toward the Lord Jesus Christ.

Water Baptism for the Remission of Sins

Once a person has thoroughly repented, he is ready to be baptized. Baptism is necessary to salvation. "He that believeth and is baptized shall be saved; but he that believeth not shall be damned" (Mark 16:16). The apostle Peter in Acts 10 commanded Cornelius and his household to be baptized although they had already received the Holy Ghost. If baptism were not necessary, he would never have commanded them to receive it. Acts 10:48 records, "And he commanded them to be baptized in the name of the Lord."

It has already been stressed to you by apostolic preaching and guidance that it is extremely important how you are baptized. Jesus gave explicit instruction in Luke 24:47 that repentance and remission of sins (water baptism) should be preached in His name. The apostles adhered to the instructions of our Lord without exception. In every place that records what was said over converts in baptism in the New Testament church, the apostles always used the name of the Lord Jesus Christ. It is for this reason that you were baptized in that name. In Acts 22:16, the apostle Paul recounted his conversion and the instructions of Ananias. "And now why tarriest thou? arise, and be baptized, and wash away thy sins, calling on the name of the Lord."

Through baptism, sins are washed away! You have been baptized in Jesus' name, and now your sins are gone. When you were baptized, the Lord washed them away, never to be remembered against you. What a thrilling experience!

The Baptism of the Holy Ghost

When one has repented of his sins and has been baptized in the name of Jesus, he will receive the gift of the Holy Ghost as declared in Acts 2:38-39. The baptism of the Holy Ghost is the greatest gift that God ever gave to a person. There is no experience in the world more exciting and thrilling than receiving the Holy Ghost.

The Holy Ghost is not only wonderful, but it is also necessary for salvation. "Jesus answered, Verily, verily, I say unto thee, Except a man be born of water and of the Spirit, he cannot enter into the kingdom of God" (John 3:5). Romans 8:9 emphasizes the necessity of receiving the Holy Ghost: "But ye are not in the flesh, but in the Spirit, if so be that the Spirit of God dwell in you. Now if any man have not the Spirit of Christ, he is none of his."

Philippians 1:19 refers to the Holy Ghost as the Spirit of Jesus Christ. When one receives the baptism of the Holy Ghost, the Spirit of the living God takes up residence in his heart. The Holy Ghost is the Spirit of God that comes to dwell in us and walk with us. Real life begins when we receive the Holy Ghost.

You have become the temple or dwelling place of the Lord Jesus. What an honor and glorious experience this is!

All Because of Calvary

This brand-new life you have just begun has been made possible by Calvary. "And that he might reconcile both unto God in one body by the cross, having slain the enmity thereby" (Ephesians 2:16). You could not enjoy this great salvation if Jesus had not paid the price for it by the shedding of His blood on Calvary. He took the hand of humanity and joined it to the hand of God.

Calvary is the story of the death, burial, and resurrection of Jesus Christ. Calvary must become our experience. We must die (repent), be buried (baptized in water), and be resurrected (be filled with the Holy Ghost). "Know ye not, that so many of us as were baptized into Jesus

Christ were baptized into his death? Therefore we are buried with him by baptism into death: that like as Christ was raised from the dead by the glory of the Father, even so we also should walk in newness of life" (Romans 6:3-4). Certainly, Calvary will ever be dear to the heart of those who really appreciate their new life and salvation!

CHAPTER 2

Learning to Walk

Your New Relationship with God

Welcome into the family of God! Now that you have been born into this family, the greatest experiences that humans can know are available to you. You have become a new spiritual creation, and you are now ready for spiritual growth. Salvation is not an end in itself; rather it is a gate through which one enters into many more new, exciting experiences.

Wouldn't it be sad indeed for a child to be born into a natural family and fail to grow? Suppose you had a child who at age six was still unable to walk or to feed himself. You would find yourself searching for the most capable physician available to diagnose his problem. Jesus compared the salvation experience to a new birth. His advice to Nicodemus was, "Ye must be born again" (John 3:7).

Now that you are a new babe in Christ, there are certain initial principles you must learn to get started in your walk with the Lord. A new baby begins the learning process immediately. He grasps, learns to focus his eyes, and becomes aware of new sounds.

Your initial spiritual steps will not be difficult. The Lord is a patient and loving Father. However, you will probably become discouraged and frustrated at times. The devil will try to prey upon you, to conquer you, to afflict, torment, and discourage you in your first important steps. I Peter 5:8 warns, "Your adversary the devil, as a roaring lion, walketh about, seeking whom he may devour."

Walking with God consists of several simple matters that God's Word clearly prescribes. The apostle Paul advised, "Be not children in understanding" (I Corinthians 14:20). Paul indicates that one cannot remain an infant. There are certain disciplines in the Christian life of which all must be aware. The Christian experience will be what we make it.

Essentials in Walking with God

1. Prayer

Very early in the life of a natural child, he learns to communicate with his parents. The first attempt may be a certain kind of cry or facial expression. No one but the parent is able to understand these feeble attempts at speech. Similarly, the new Christian must begin to communicate with his Father. This is accomplished through prayer (communion with God).

When you pray, talk to God as you would your natural father or a respected friend and advisor. You will find that He is interested in the daily problems you face. These first attempts at prayer may be feeble, but this does not matter. God looks at your heart. He is able to discern your thoughts.

Without a doubt, prayer is one of the most vital matters in your walk with God. Without it you will soon die spiritually. You should have a certain time to pray, a definite hour in which to go before your heavenly Father. Do not be casual about your prayer life, praying only when it is convenient. The casual, intermittent prayer is never bathed in divine fire. One who prays in this manner lacks in earnestness and effectiveness. God wants to be the most important one in your daily schedule. Learn to put God first in your time while you are still a young Christian. The conflicts ahead will be far easier if you practice this valuable lesson.

2. Fasting

Christ instructed us to fast and pray. During a fast, we

sacrifice the natural to emphasize the spiritual. It is not something we do because others are doing it. Rather, it is a tool to help keep our body under subjection. Fasting and praying gives the spiritual man an opportunity to talk to God and to feast on His goodness. Jesus gave instructions relative to fasting in Matthew 6:16-18.

3. Reading the Scripture

King David declared, "Thy word is a lamp unto my feet, and a light unto my path" (Psalm 119:105). Paul instructed Timothy, "Study to shew thyself approved unto God, a workman that needeth not to be ashamed, rightly dividing the word of truth" (II Timothy 2:15). In the discussion of the early development of a Christian, we cannot minimize the importance of reading the Word.

You should have a systematic approach in studying the Bible. Do not skip around from one book to the next.

A good place to start is the Gospel of John. Read it through several times until you become familiar with Christ as John knew Him. Follow this by reading the other Gospels through once or more (Matthew, Mark, and Luke). By starting with the Gospels, you will feed your soul upon the Lord's words and deeds. Look long into His face. Next, read the New Testament through. As you continue your reading, you may want to delve into other parts of Scripture, such as the Psalms or Genesis (the book of beginnings). By reading three chapters daily and five on Sunday, you will be able to read through the Bible in one year.

Determine to hide the Word deep in your heart. Such an attitude will keep you from temptation and failure. The psalmist knew this, for he wrote, "Thy word have I hid in mine heart, that I might not sin against thee" (Psalm 119:11).

In addition to being systematic in your reading you must also be regular. You now have a new life in you—a spiritual life. The Word of God nourishes this spiritual life just as bread nourishes your natural body. Spasmodic reading of the Word will result in spiritual malnutrition. Do not let a day go by without reading some portion of

Scripture. Jesus said, "Man shall not live by bread alone, but by every word that proceedeth out of the mouth of God" (Matthew 4:4). Begin at once the practice of daily reading.

Private reading is not your only opportunity to digest the Word. Your church will provide you with the privilege of hearing the Word taught and preached. After you return home from a Bible study, look up the passages of Scripture used and read them again. This will provide additional food for your soul. Studies show that ninety percent of the material reviewed within twenty-four hours is retained. However, with no review, ninety percent is lost.

4. Witnessing

Another great step in the Christian life is witnessing. Acts 1:8 tells us, "But ye shall receive power, after that the Holy Ghost is come upon you: and ye shall be witnesses." The power to witness comes to everyone who is filled with the Spirit. To witness does not mean that you will be a preacher or that you are instantly experienced or profound in the Scriptures. Witnessing is simply relating your experience to someone else, telling what God has done in your life. A witness testifies only about things he knows. In a court trial, a witness is someone who relates the facts as he experienced them.

In your witnessing, do not emphasize negative aspects. Be careful not to focus on dos and don'ts or to attack the beliefs of others. Keep a positive outlook in your witness. You will be surprised at how easy it is to become an effective instrument in the Lord's work.

Later you may want to obtain some of the special tools and soulwinning helps available through your church and join with other soulwinners in a planned effort to reach others.

5. Faithfulness

　　a. Attendance to God's house

The writer of the Book of Hebrews charged, "And let us consider one another to provoke unto love and to good works: not forsaking the assembling of ourselves together, as the manner of some is; but exhorting one another: and so much the more, as ye see the day approaching" (Hebrews 10:24-25). Worshiping the Lord in His house is an important source of spiritual nourishment. Missing a service would be like missing a natural meal at home. When the lady of the house announces that a meal is ready, we immediately go to eat. We do not say, "That meal is not for us." Every church service is important and must be attended. This includes Sunday school, Sunday evening service, Bible study, youth service, prayer meeting, and revival services. There is no such thing as a big or a little service.

God speaks through the ministry, letting us know what we must do. Failure to attend services leaves a person without direction in his life. Paul said, "That we henceforth be no more children, tossed to and fro, and carried about with every wind of doctrine, by the sleight of men, and cunning craftiness, whereby they lie in wait to deceive" (Ephesians 4:14). If we are to develop stability in our lives we must know the Word. We cannot really know the Word without hearing it. In his letter to the Romans Paul posed the question, "And how shall they hear without a preacher?" (Romans 10:14). Ignorance of the Word leaves us open to false doctrine. We can prevent this problem by faithfulness to the house of God. God has called pastors, evangelists, and teachers that we might hear and believe the Word.

b. Giving

Part of our responsibility to God is to give of our finances to the work of the Lord. Let us be generous givers. The pocketbook is often a sensitive spot. Surprisingly, many people lose their religious sentiments when money is mentioned. Giving is an attitude of worship, and we will be blessed by participating.

Our Lord had much to say on this subject. "Give, and it shall be given unto you; good measure, pressed down, and shaken together, and running over, shall men give into your bosom" (Luke 6:38). "But lay up for yourselves treasures in heaven, where neither moth nor rust doth corrupt, and where thieves do not break through nor steal: for where your treasure is, there will your heart be also" (Matthew 6:20).

The Bible speaks of tithes and offerings (Malachi 3:8-10). The tithe is ten percent of our earnings, and it goes for the support of the ministry and the spreading of the gospel. (Chapter 4 covers the subject of tithing in greater depth.) Offerings include many areas of giving. The local church may have several projects as well as supporting the international efforts of the United Pentecostal Church.

We must learn to give freely—from the heart. "For God loveth a cheerful giver" (II Corinthians 9:7). One who has learned the secret of giving has learned the secret of prospering. We are taught in the Bible that we reap what we sow; so to reap big dividends, we must give accordingly. If we sow little, we will reap little. Conversely, if we sow much, we will reap much.

c. Involvement

As a natural child grows he becomes more and more a part of the family unit. This is also true of the new Christian. He must become involved in the Lord's family.

Do not be a bystander or an onlooker in your new walk with God. Make yourself available to do whatever your pastor asks you to do. Involvement makes one a part of the church family. Volunteer your services with a free and willing heart to do what needs to be done.

What If I Stumble?

We all make mistakes in our relationship with the Lord. The devil will place opposition in your way. You may lose your balance and even fall. It is all a part of learning to walk. But this is no time to quit. Remember that Christ has given His life for you. "My little children, these things write I unto you, that ye sin not. And if any man sin, we have an advocate with the Father, Jesus Christ the righteous: and he is the propitiation for our sins: and not for ours only, but also for the sins of the whole world" (I John 2:1-2).

When you make a mistake, go to your heavenly Father in repentance and confession. He is always waiting to restore you to a full relationship with Himself. The enemy will try to make you believe that because you have made a mistake, it is all over. The devil is described in the Bible as the "prince and power of the air." His objective is to bring down every soul. The Holy Ghost gives us power to be victorious over Satan. "Greater is he that is in you, than he that is in the world" (I John 4:4). Should you fall, get up! God will strengthen you in every way. The Lord wants to take your hand and lead you.

Yes, your first steps with the Lord are simple ones, but they are vital to further maturity. Paul said, "When I was a child, I spake as a child, I understood as a child, I thought as a child: but when I became a man, I put away childish things" (I Corinthians 13:11). The Christian life is a forward progression, a growing-up process. You should not remain a child. You must grow up. You must follow God's precepts, talking with Him and letting God deal with you. If you are to be victorious, you must carefully consider the steps that you have read in this chapter.

CHAPTER 3

Encountering Conflict from Satan

Everything in life has an enemy. As a new Christian, you are no exception. You will not go far on this pilgrim journey until you meet opposition, both from within and without.

Salvation is a joyous experience! The prophet Isaiah declared, "With joy shall ye draw water out of the wells of salvation" (Isaiah 12:13). The apostle Paul wrote to the Romans, "Now the God of hope fill you with all joy . . . in believing" (Romans 15:13). Joy is a fruit of the Spirit (Galatians 5:22). Every born-again believer can expect to experience joy, God's joy, in believing, and at times it may be rapturous.

Sometimes, however, without warning, that rapturous joy can turn into heaviness, even to the extent of spiritual depression. Overnight, the wells seem to dry up. "Where did it go?" you may ask. "How did it slip away? From where did this feeling of heaviness come? Have I lost the wonderful salvation that yesterday I so thoroughly enjoyed? Yesterday, the exuberance seemed unbelievable; today it is but a memory. Could it have been an illusion? What happened?"

Satan has entered the scene. Not knowing the Word of God and unaware that Satan is attacking them, many new Christians have thrown in the towel at this point. Had they known what to expect from Satan, and that wonderful victory could be theirs through the Lord Jesus Christ, they would have held on to God and would not have given up so quickly.

Remember this whenever you are attacked by Satan: regardless from whom or where it comes, the conflict is between God and Satan. Jesus Christ came into the world to secure a final victory over Satan, and there remains one final bout with him to accomplish that purpose!

What Jesus Faced after His Baptism

While Christ was here on the earth He faced Satan in two major battles. One was immediately after His baptism, the other at Calvary. Thank God, He was the victor both times! He will be the victor in the last bout also, as John recorded in Revelation 20:1-10.

When Jesus emerged from the waters of baptism, He did not begin His wonderful ministry immediately. Instead He went directly into the wilderness. The Scripture says that the Spirit led Him to the wilderness (Luke 4:1). We learn from this example that when we are directed by the Spirit, we will not always face pleasant things. Rather, we will often find ourselves in hot water, sometimes up to our necks!

When someone gives his heart to the Lord and is born again of the water and Spirit, he becomes a son of God (Romans 8:14-18; I John 3:1-3). As Satan challenged the Sonship of Christ, so will he challenge our being a son of God, a joint-heir with Christ.

Satan's challenge to Christ was three pronged. "If thou be the Son of God . . ." was the beginning statement of Satan on two of the temptations. At the other temptation, where he showed Christ all the kingdoms of the world and asserted that he (Satan) had jurisdiction over them, he declared, "All of this power will I give thee . . . if thou therefore wilt worship me, all shall be thine" (Luke 4:6-7).

By quoting what was written in the Word, Jesus successfully rebuffed Satan and came out of the wilderness victorious! He faced Satan with, "It is written. . . ." This response was His victory, and it will be yours!

Satan's tempting of you will probably be different from the way he tempted Christ, but rest assured, he will attack you! Nevertheless, also remain certain that the Lord will be with you, and through Him you can overcome anything Satan thrusts at you!

Satan will attack you from without and within. From without he will use people. From within he will appeal to the lust of the flesh, the lust of the eyes, and the pride of life (I John 2:16).

People need not necessarily be demon-possessed to be used by Satan. He will at times use good people, even disciples of the Lord, to frustrate you.

An instance of this occurred in the life of the apostle Peter. The Lord chose him to receive and use the keys of the kingdom. But Satan used this chosen vessel when he rebuked the Lord for saying that He would go to Jerusalem, suffer many things, be killed, and rise on the third day. Jesus recognized who was behind this rebuke of Peter's and spoke to him, "Get thee behind me, Satan: thou art an offence unto me: for thou savourest not the things that be of God, but those that be of men" (Matthew 16:23). Because the apostle Peter did not understand, he could be used of Satan. And yet he was unaware of what was happening.

Yes, Satan will use people to attempt to deter you from doing the will of God for your life. Recognize the source of the discouragement, and do not allow yourself to blame people for your fall or failure.

Satan may appeal to your pride and tell you that you are stronger than you really are. He did this to Peter just before Peter denied Christ three times. Peter made a show of his strength and bravery by declaring that he was willing to die for and with Christ. But a few moments later he faced the prospect of fulfilling his word, and he turned traitor. He denied Jesus. His pride overruled his better judgment when he so boldly asserted his strength. When he heard the rooster crow, he recognized how foolish he had been to listen to Satan and to yield to such a boasting spirit (Luke 22:31-62).

Satan will attempt to infiltrate your mind with his evil. In John 13:2 Satan put it into the heart of Judas to betray the Lord Jesus Christ. If there is one thing we should guard with all of our lives, it is our honesty before God. If Judas had been honest with himself and with God, Satan would never have been able to put such thoughts into his heart.

We must guard diligently what goes into our minds! Through one means or another Satan will try to get evil there. What we see, hear, feel, taste, and smell, enters our mind. We should never listen to malicious gossip that may float around among church members. Satan will use it to poison our thinking. We should carefully guard what we read and watch . . . for here is another entrance for his evil!

The apostle Paul told the Romans to renew their minds (Romans 12:1-2); the only way you can do so is by rejecting constantly and consistently those evil thoughts that at one time may have possessed you. You must adopt a whole new thought pattern. You must work out a new schedule of feeding the mind with the good things of God. That is why you must keep yourself in church as much as humanly possible. Read the Word of God every day, study and meditate upon it, fast and pray regularly; by doing these things you will constantly renew your mind with good things.

Paul gave the church in Philippi a thought pattern that every Christian should make a part of his life. In Philippians 4:6-8 he admonished us to give ourselves to prayer and supplication and promised that when we do, the peace of God will keep our heart and mind through Christ Jesus. Then he gave eight themes for thought: "Whatsoever things are true, whatsoever things are honest, whatsoever things are just, whatsoever things are pure, whatsoever things are lovely, whatsoever things are of good report; if there be any virtue, and if there be any praise, think on these things."

Fill your mind with these things instead of the trash

you may see or hear. This takes conscious effort, but it will pay big dividends later on in your Christian life and thwart the effort of Satan to put evil into your heart.

You must not minimize Satan's power. "Your adversary the devil, as a roaring lion, walketh about, seeking whom he may devour" (I Peter 5:8). Peter exhorted us to be sober, vigilant, and ready to resist the devil steadfastly! James said, "Submit yourselves therefore to God. Resist the devil, and he will flee from you" (James 4:7). The key to resisting the devil and having him flee from you is submission to God. The next verse says, "Draw nigh to God, and he will draw nigh to you" (James 4:8).

Satan cannot defeat you or detour you from the will of God if you will keep yourself in the love of God by submission to Him! Remember this, and victory will always be yours in the Lord!

What Israel Faced

There is an Old Testament event that foreshadowed the plan of salvation as outlined in the New Testament. This was the release and subsequent journey of Israel out of the land of Egypt and to Canaan, the Promised Land.

Israel was in deep bondage and cried for deliverance. God heard their cry and sent Moses. Moses met stiff opposition in his endeavor to win release for his people, but finally God intervened in a most remarkable way.

God commanded Israel to kill the Passover lamb, catch the blood in a basin, and then sprinkle it on the door posts and lintels of their homes. After this they were to retire inside, prepare the lamb for a meal, and make ready for a journey.

They did as God commanded. Pharaoh released the Israelites, and they were on their way to the Promised Land. Everything was going fine, and what a happy band of people they were. Finally, after all those years, they were free. All they had done was believe and obey what God had asked them to do, and God did the rest.

But then something happened! The cloud they were

following, which was to direct and also protect them, led them to a peculiar place. It was between two mountains, with the Red Sea directly ahead. When they could go no further because of the sea, they looked back to discover the Egyptian army pursuing them. They became panic-stricken! Pharaoh was coming to return them to bondage. They had not anticipated this and were not prepared for it. Up to this point everything had gone so well. Now what was to happen?

This was their first big test, and their reaction was not too pleasant. They cried out to Moses and blamed him. Had they forgotten so soon that it was God who was leading them?

Just when they thought it was a lost cause, God performed a miracle of deliverance. And let us remember, He loves us every bit as much as He did them! The cloud that led them and brought them to this place moved to the rear and cut them off from the Egyptians. Then God opened the Red Sea, allowing the Israelites to march across on dry land. When the Egyptians tried to do the same they were swallowed up by the same waters (Exodus 6:1-15, 27).

As we continue reading this account we find that God did many wonderful things for these people, all designed to make them aware that He was leading them and would take care of them. The only thing they needed to fear was themselves. God was their Savior, keeper, guide and master. Everything they would ever need, He provided.

You Will Face Similar Experiences

From this story you can glean a wonderful truth: God will see you through every trial and hard place. In fact, He probably is allowing you to get into a hard place to show Himself strong on your behalf. If you will be patient, trusting, and willing to obey Him, you will overcome every temptation and test that Satan puts in your pathway. Read the wonderful promise of God in I Corinthians 10:1-13, and note very carefully that God will always give you "a way to escape, that ye may be able to bear it." God will never allow any trial to come in your direction unless there is a way out! If you are going through a difficult place, rest upon the promise of this verse. It belongs to you!

I Peter 1:6 is a special verse of Scripture filled with meaning for someone who is undergoing a time of severe trial or temptation. The apostle described the wonderful salvation of the Lord Jesus and declared that we have been saved "to an inheritance incorruptible, and undefiled, and that fadeth not away, reserved in heaven for you, who are kept by the power of God through faith unto salvation ready to be revealed in the last time" (I Peter 1:4-5). He said that these things were the basis of great rejoicing. To know that we have reservations in a place that is incorruptible and undefiled . . . that will not vanish away like the mist in the morning sun . . . is a matter of consolation. Then he introduced another subject, one of difficulty, when he said, "Though now for a season, if need be, ye are in heaviness through manifold temptations" (I Peter 1:6).

Study carefully the phrase "if need be." Could it be that the Lord, knowing us better than we know ourselves, sometimes leads us into difficult circumstances that are necessary for our spiritual growth?

If you will ask yourself, "Why am I going through such a trial?" in light of this verse of Scripture, perhaps you will see the reason.

Most of us have had trials that perplexed us. At the time we could not understand the reason why we were called upon to go through them. However, a few years later as we looked back over the events, they all made sense. If nothing more, we find praise and honor and glory at the appearing of the Lord Jesus Christ, if we have stood the test (I Peter 1:7). That is reason enough for a Christian to follow as God leads.

How Victory Comes

Strength comes through struggle! Victory comes only when you fully surrender to the Lord. Often you will think you have fully surrendered, until He asks you to give up something you do not want to give up.

This is when prayer and fasting become powerful forces in your life. Prayer and fasting do not move God nearly as much as they move you. If you are in the perfect will of God, you will lay on the altar the things that hinder you, and God knows what they are. A fervent prayer meeting will make you willing for the Lord to have His way in your life. You see, God knows the end from the beginning. While you are still playing the game, He knows what the score will be! That is why we need to trust Him with everything in life. Someone who tosses in the towel and draws back does so because he did not yield some part of his life to God.

Reread the stories surrounding the temptation of the Lord and the deliverance of Israel out of Egypt; then determine to follow where the Lord leads. These things happened as examples for us and were written for our admonition (I Corinthians 10:11).

Resist Satan with positive action—the action of faith and trust. Confess, "God is taking me through this trial, and by His grace I'll make it." Do not even think about defeat! Think only of the promises of God and victory.

Read stories of personal deliverance, such as those of Daniel and the three young Hebrews (Daniel 3:1-30; 6:1-28). Read how Paul was delivered so many times (II Corinthians 11:23-28). Yet remember that at the end of his life he was beheaded for the name of Jesus Christ. Accept what happens to you as the will of God and allow Him to lead you. He is faithful! His Word says it! (I Corinthians 1:9). Some suffering may be necessary in your life, but it cannot be compared with the glory that will be revealed at His coming (II Corinthians 4:16-18).

Finally, never forget the wonderful promise of I Corinthians 10:13. There is a way of escape in every temptation and trial. Just wait and God will reveal it!

CHAPTER 4

Your Church and You

What is the church? Often the term *church* is used to refer to a particular building or organization, but these are not really the church.

The church is a body of baptized believers, molded and welded together through the Spirit of God. "Now therefore ye are no more strangers and foreigners, but fellow-citizens with the saints, and of the household of God; and are built upon the foundation of the apostles and prophets, Jesus Christ himself being the chief corner stone; in whom all the building fitly framed together groweth unto an holy temple in the Lord: in whom ye also are builded together for an habitation of God through the Spirit" (Ephesians 2:19-22). According to I Corinthians 6:19-20, we become the temple of the Holy Ghost when we are filled with the Spirit of God. We are then blended spiritually with those of the local congregation where we worship, thus composing an effective unit to do the work of the kingdom of God in our locale.

We must always remember, however, that our local assembly is not the total church. Our local assembly joins with hundreds of other assemblies of like precious faith to make a globe-girdling church. The church is the worldwide body of people who have been baptized in Jesus' name, have received the Holy Spirit, and are living holy and godly lives. The church also includes people who have already gone by the way of the grave and are waiting for the soon return of our Lord Jesus Christ.

Respect for Leadership

Let us consider your personal involvement in the local church. One element of prime importance, if you are to work in harmony with the local congregation, is a deep respect for leadership. The most important of all your leaders will be your pastor. According to the Word of God, you owe him your honor, loyalty, and obedience. He is the shepherd of your soul. The Bible instructs, "Obey them that have the rule over you, and submit yourselves; for they watch for your souls, as they that must give account, that they may do it with joy, and not with grief: for that is unprofitable for you" (Hebrews 13:17). The quickest way to bring spiritual failure to your life is to rebel against the person whom God has placed over you as pastor.

Under the pastor of the church, there will be other leaders in varying positions with different degrees of responsibility. If you are sincere about your walk with God, you will do everything in your power to work in harmony with each of them. In all your relationships, however, it is wise to remember that the pastor is the final spiritual authority under God in the local church.

From time to time, your church will be blessed with the ministry of visiting ministers, including evangelists, Bible teachers, and organizational leaders. You owe these people of God the honor and respect of which their office and work are worthy. They cannot fill the role of your pastor, however. He is the one to whom you should go for spiritual advice and counsel. Your pastor is the most important person in your relationship with God. Honor, love, and trust him in all matters.

Church Attendance

You have some responsibilities to God and to your local church. The first of these is faithfulness in church attendance. This is of vital importance according to Hebrews 10:25: "Not forsaking the assembling of ourselves together, as the manner of some is, but exhorting one another: and so much the more, as you see the day approaching." You can never hope to have total victory in your Christian walk and be ready for the second coming of Christ if you are not faithful in church attendance.

At the beginning, you make habits; in the end, habits make you. By refusing to allow anything to hinder your church attendance at the outset of your Christian walk, faithfulness will tend to characterize your entire walk with God. You will become one of "the faithful," and you will know the joy of being used of God. Growth in grace and knowledge will be yours. Church attendance is a must!

Tithes and Offerings

Another responsibility and great privilege is giving to the cause of God. God loves a cheerful giver (II Corinthians 9:7). Your giving of finances to the kingdom of God will fall into two categories. The first of these is tithing. Tithing is not a plan instituted by humans, but rather by Almighty God. The word *tithe* means one tenth. Tithing, consequently, is the giving of the first tenth of your income to the Lord.

Malachi 3:8-10 teaches: "Will a man rob God? Yet ye have robbed me. But ye say, Wherein have we robbed thee? In tithes and offerings. Ye are cursed with a curse: for ye have robbed me, even this whole nation. Bring ye all the tithes into the storehouse, that there may be meat in mine house, and prove me now herewith, saith the LORD of hosts, if I will not open you the windows of heaven, and pour you out a blessing, that there shall not be room enough to receive it." God's command is, "Bring ye all the tithes," and He accuses these who fail to do so of robbing God.

You are to give your tithing into your local church. It is not to be sent across the country or to be used for other charitable donations. According to the Scriptures, the first purpose of tithing is the support of the ministry.

Tithing is a commandment with great promise. The

Lord said He would open the windows of heaven and pour out such a blessing that there would not be room enough to receive it.

The second classification of financial giving is offerings. There is no set amount for offerings. They are strictly free will and voluntary. However, the Lord promises that the more liberal we are with Him, the more we shall be blessed in return. We should not try to get by on giving as little as possible but rather should endeavor to give as much as possible to the cause of the Lord Jesus. If we really love God and His cause, we will not find it difficult to give, and give generously, to His work.

Personal Witnessing

Another very important responsibility is personal witnessing. Jesus instructed His disciples concerning this vital Christian function just prior to His ascension into heaven. "But ye shall receive power, after that the Holy Ghost is come upon you: and ye shall be witnesses unto me both in Jerusalem, and in all Judaea, and in Samaria, and unto the uttermost part of the earth" (Acts 1:8). Your spiritual life will become stagnant and eventually shrivel and die if you do not cultivate the art of witnessing. But if you cultivate that art, your life will take on new meaning. You will see lives changed, souls saved, the sick healed, and miracles happen. Your personal witness is powerful. No one else can give it for you. It is yours; it is personal.

You Need the Church

Never be guilty of thinking that you can be saved without the church. The fellowship, friendship, encouragement, and testimonies of fellow saints do much to strengthen your own spiritual walk with God. You will quickly learn that we really need each other. None of us is self-sufficient. The saints in the church will be your greatest friends on this earth.

There are other elements of great value in the church that make it essential to our spiritual success. The worship serves to lift and strengthen the child of God. The preached and taught Word of God during the services becomes our food and source of encouragement and faith. The work of the ministry is a most vital link in God's overall plan of salvation. Yes, my friend, you need the church!

Involvement with the District and International Church

Your local church is involved with district programs as well as the work of God in your own city. These include activities such as rallies, youth camps, camp meetings, and conferences, where saints and ministers of many local assemblies gather to worship and to gain an increased vision and burden for the work of the Lord.

Local churches are encouraged to be involved with other assemblies of like precious faith, not only on a district level but also nationally and worldwide. For this purpose, we have an organization called the United Pentecostal Church International. It was formed by a merger of two organizations in 1945. Its current headquarters, known as World Evangelism Center, is located in the St. Louis area at 8855 Dunn Road, Hazelwood, Missouri.

Each year the United Pentecostal Church International holds an annual general conference, convening in various cities. Saints and ministers from all over America, Canada, and around the world come to worship together and to share visions and burdens with each other. It is a great time of fellowship and spiritual feasting.

The United Pentecostal Church International has organized its ministries under several divisions. These include Church Administration, Editorial, Education, Foreign Missions, Harvestime (radio ministry), Home Missions, Pentecostal Publishing House, Women's, Sunday School, and Youth.

The Foreign Missions Division raises finances to support missionaries around the world through Faith Promise (personal faith commitments) and distributes the money through Partners in Missions (monthly pledges to particular missionaries). The Home Missions Division starts churches in cities of the United States and Canada where there is no lighthouse of truth, and its fundraising effort is called Christmas for Christ. The Youth Division conducts many forms of youth ministry. Its financial drive, known as Sheaves for Christ, not only sponsors youth projects but also buys vehicles for our missionaries. The Women's Division receives a Mother's Memorial offering each year. Among other things, it supports foreign Bible school students and purchases appliances for our missionaries. The Sunday School Division, using its Save Our Children offering, sponsors ministries for children and helps pay for the education of our missionary children.

There are many other projects that space will not permit us to mention. The goal behind each of them is the conquest of unreached territory and the winning of lost souls for the kingdom of God. The work of God on this earth is no small task. It demands a worldwide effort.

Each church cannot do a tremendous amount in all these areas by itself, but when many assemblies join together their efforts become very effective. This is why your local church is involved with district and national programs.

Your Secret for Success

There is a secret to successful Christian living. That secret is total involvement in everything possible within the framework of the local church. Exhaust every possible avenue of doing something for God and working in His kingdom, and your new life will continue to be filled with victory, excitement and great joy!

CHAPTER 5

The World and You

Getting the World in Proper Perspective

What do the world and the Christian have in common? Two Bible quotations provide the answer. "Love not the world, neither the things that are in the world. If any man love the world, the love of the Father is not in him. For all that is in the world, the lust of the flesh, and the lust of the eyes, and the pride of life, is not of the Father, but is of the world" (I John 2:15-17). "Ye adulterers and adulteresses, know ye not that the friendship of the world is enmity with God? whosoever therefore will be a friend of the world is the enemy of God" (James 4:4).

In these passages, the "world" refers to the ungodly system that holds the earth in its sway. When Satan tempted Christ in the wilderness, he paraded before Him all the kingdoms of the world in a moment of time. In his clever attempt to thwart the plan of God, he insidiously associated with the world two powerful forces that are especially attractive to people: power and glory (Luke 4:6). Further, he intimated slyly that these forces were at his disposal and dispensable at his will.

If Satan possesses such ability, certainly it is reasonable to suggest that a new convert needs to be on constant alert. Satan is sure to dangle these two alluring attractions before him in an attempt to frustrate his life and hinder his progress in the Lord.

Christians often refer to certain things one says,

wears, or does as being "worldly," meaning that it belongs to the world's values or system, which is influenced and controlled by satanic forces. The new convert should be reticent to partake of or participate in anything that threatens to involve him with, or make him a slave to, this system. Of necessity, we must live in this world, yet we must be as pilgrims and strangers to it (Hebrews 11:13).

The apostle Paul instructed, "Abstain from all appearance of evil" (I Thessalonians 5:22). We are to shun everything that could be construed as evil and disassociate ourselves from questionable practices that Satan could take advantage of. He longs for this type of influence in our lives (II Corinthians 2:11). Courting doubtful practices may well cause us to become entangled in the things of the world.

Paul commanded Timothy, "Flee also youthful lusts" (II Timothy 2:22). The Living Bible paraphrases, "Run from anything that gives you the evil thoughts that young men often have, but stay close to anything that makes you want to do right."

These passages of Scripture indicate that the individual Christian has power to refrain or to participate, to run or to stay. Too often, people expect God to keep them from questionable or dangerous things, but this thinking is erroneous. The power to do or refrain from doing is within our own will, given by the anointing of the Holy Spirit and the knowledge of the Word of God.

Paul stated this truth clearly in instructing the church at Rome. "Let not sin therefore reign in your mortal body, that ye should obey it in the lusts thereof. . . . Neither yield ye your members as instruments of unrighteousness unto sin: but yield yourselves unto God, as those that are alive from the dead, and your members as instruments of righteousness unto God. . . . Know ye not, that to whom ye yield yourselves servants to obey, his servants ye are to whom ye obey; whether of sin unto death, or of obedience unto righteousness?" (Romans 6:12, 13, 16).

To put it bluntly, you are at the controls, holding your

destiny in your own hands. You must come to grips with the world and recognize it for the evil system that it is! "And the world passeth away, and the lusts thereof" (I John 2:17). Therefore, in any association you have with it, you must keep this perspective in mind.

Participation in Questionable Activities

In many areas, a thin line separates right from wrong. Separation from the world is not always easy and is sometimes difficult to explain to someone who has had little or no spiritual background. Some things we will address on this subject could be controversial. Since the Bible does not deal with every specific contingency of evil, especially involving modern innovations, we must ascertain the general principles of the Word of God and then make practical applications to our own time, place, and circumstances.

Let us take, for instance, the practice of smoking. There are no obvious references to smoking in the Bible, but is it right for a Christian to indulge in it? There are scriptural principles from which we can obtain guidance and draw a reasonable conclusion.

1. Drinking, Smoking, and Drug Use

The Scriptures are not silent on the practice of drinking. It is wrong because it leads to drunkenness and addiction, both of which the Bible condemns. This habit leads many to despair, disgrace, and destruction. In one study of 882 criminal arrests, 72.7 percent of the crimes involved alcohol in some measure.

The following passages of Scripture will reveal God's viewpoint on the subject: Deuteronomy 21:20; Proverbs 20:1; 23:20, 29-35; Isaiah 5:11, 28:1; Habakkuk 2:15; Luke 21:34; Romans 13:13; I Corinthians 6:10; Ephesians 5:18.

Certainly no genuine Christian should indulge in such a questionable, addictive habit that has destroyed so many homes and ruined so many lives. It should be one of the first things to go when one obeys the Scriptures and gives his life to God!

Should a Christian smoke? Almost immediately, the adherents to this addictive habit loudly proclaim, "There is no direct Scripture that prohibits it." Granted, that is true. There is no direct reference to smoking anywhere in the Bible. However, the practice is entirely contradictory to the spirit of the Scripture, which teaches, "All things are lawful unto me, but all things are not expedient: all things are lawful for me, but I will not be brought under the power of any" (I Corinthians 6:12). The use of tobacco in any form is addictive. It is a filthy habit and intrudes into the privacy of others who do not indulge. It holds one tenaciously in its grip. Many loudly proclaim that they can stop whenever they desire, but few of them ever do.

It is a health hazard—so much of one, in fact, that the government severly restricts its advertising and every pack of cigarettes carries a sober warning of danger printed on it. Should a Christian partake of something so flagrantly destructive and injurious? The answer is obviously no.

The twentieth century added another treacherous scourge to the already overcrowded scene: drugs! As if the other prevalent addictive substances were not enough, Satan has added this curse against the sanctity of human life, the authority of God, and the decency of society.

This scourge has even invaded the religious scene. Some have claimed that using drugs has spiritual value. Some have supposedly gained new insights into both self and God while high on drugs. However, no one under the influence of such an intoxicating force could possibly see things correctly. It is an illusion, and the experiences are merely hallucinations. Such practices are foreign to the Word of God and should be avoided as evil by every convert.

The individual who needs such an artificial means of inducing a "spiritual" experience is certainly unaware of the biblical teaching of the mighty power of the Holy Spirit in one's life. Jesus Christ, living within one through the infusion of the Holy Spirit, adequately meets the need of penitent, sincere individuals without any artificial inducement.

2. Dancing, Parties, and Mixed Swimming

The modern dance was not designed to glorify God. Regardless of the form it takes, its appeal is to the lower nature of humanity. Its lure is to the lust of the flesh and is purely physical in its excitement. The music is usually suggestive and the atmosphere conducive to wrong motives.

No Christian belongs on the worldly dance floor. The body of the Christian belongs to the Lord, is His temple, and should never be made a party to the evil associated with the dance. We were bought with a very dear price, the blood of Jesus Christ, and are therefore admonished to glorify God in our bodies (I Corinthians 6:19-20).

A party can be either good or bad. It depends on the purpose, people, and place. Where will it be held? Who will be there? What will go on? Will it be supervised? It is certainly not wrong to have good, wholesome fun, and everyone can stand a little humor to compensate for some of the tensions experienced in the rush of this hour. Before we participate in a social activity, however, we must be sure that the purpose, place, and people are conducive to an atmosphere of Christian conduct required by the Word of God.

The Bible has never changed. Neither has the Lord. Modesty is a virtue acquired with the infusion of the Holy Spirit and required by the Word of God. It should never be compromised anytime, anywhere, or under any circumstances. The body belongs to the Lord and should not be up for auction to the lustful eyes of the world. We cannot control what goes on in the mind of the lustful, but it is entirely unnecessary for the Christian to add insult to God and humans by nudity, seminudity, or immodest exposure by improper dress.

Deep within the heart of all Pentecostal Christians should be a desire to attire themselves so that they never need be ashamed or embarrassed under any circumstances. Swimming in scanty attire at a public beach, or in private parties where there are people of the opposite sex outside the immediate family, would not fit into these circumstances. We also need to consider others who may be embarrassed because of our attire. The modern bathing suit is neither modest nor godly.

3. Recreation

Recreation is a refreshing of oneself by means of relaxation and enjoyment. Wholesome recreation is beneficial for anyone. Not all recreations are wholesome, however. The new convert should seek the advice of the pastor before participating in anything that could be questionable. There are dozens of wholesome activities that add zest and fun to life, and it is sheer delight to participate in them. No Christian need partake of questionable recreational practices when there are so many excellent things of a beneficial nature that one can participate in.

However, even right activities can become wrong when overindulged in, or when a wrong attitude develops. As an example, it was the custom in one church to have a lively, spirited softball game between the married and unmarried fellows on the day of the Sunday school picnic. The married fellows had won most of the games, so the unmarrieds set out to change the course of things. They vowed to beat the "old men" this particular year and practiced secretly to prepare themselves. Meanwhile they carried on a roasting and ribbing of the marrieds, declaring what they meant to do to them.

Finally the day of the picnic came, and the friendly game of ball turned into a heated affair when the unmarrieds, despite all their practice, were badly beaten. They became sullen and argumentative and breathed out some unkind verbiage that spoiled the game. The right turned into wrong because of the attitudes. The wise pastor discontinued the game until the proper attitudes could be regained.

4. *Organized Sports*

It has long been the general practice for members of United Pentecostal churches to refrain from participation in high school and college varsity competition and professional athletics. The reason is that participation in organized sports has serious pitfalls. Few athletes are able to keep up with the whirl of competitive sports and maintain their integrity with God. The demands on the time and talent of the individual can become pernicious, and the atmosphere of the competitions is often quite worldly. The lure of the limelight, the billboards, and the headlines can unbalance an otherwise sane and sensible youth. Often the influence of ungodly companions and roommates have a deteriorating effect on one's spiritual life. The overall results of those who have participated leaves much to be desired.

5. *Hair Length*

The Bible speaks clearly concerning the length of hair, for both men and women. I Corinthians 11 teaches definite guidelines in this area that the Christian can easily apply to his life.

This passage teaches that a woman should have long hair and not cut it. For a woman to cut her hair is a shame, as though she were shaven. Her long hair is a glory to her; it honors God and her husband and displays her obedience to the Lord.

A man's hair should be cut short. It is a dishonor to him and to his position under God and as head of his home to allow his hair to grow long. Though some paintings show Christ with long hair, we must remember that these are not photographs but the product of human imagination and do not show the facts. Long hair on a man is a shame to him.

Though fashions change from season to season, we must remain consistent with the Scripture. How a woman fixes her long hair is a matter of personal preference, but it should always be consistent with the teachings of the Bible.

6. Modest and Immodest Appearance

I Timothy 2:8-10 tells us, "I will therefore that men pray every where, lifting up holy hands, without wrath and doubting. In like manner also, that women adorn themselves in modest apparel, with shamefacedness and sobriety; not with broided hair, or gold, or pearls, or costly array; but (which becometh women professing godliness) with good works."

Being modest means "having or showing a humble estimate of one's merits, importance, etc.; free from ostentation; moderate; and decent." If people have a modest appearance, (a) they will not exalt themselves or brag on themselves; (b) they will shrink from pretentious or ostentatious display; (c) they will follow a moderate course, that is, avoiding extremes; and (d) they will seek to maintain decency in walk, talk, and dress.

Being immodest is just the opposite. The meaning of "immodest" is "indecent, shameless; forward, impudent." "Impudent" means "characterized by a shameless boldness, effrontery."

The apostle Paul confronted both male and female with the proper attitude and appearance, which sets the standard for all to follow. In the passage just quoted, he had three things to say to each sex. To the men he exhorted: (a) pray everywhere, (b) lift up holy hands, and (c) have no wrath or doubt. To the women he exhorted: (a) adorn yourselves with modest apparel, (b) adorn yourselves with shamefacedness and sobriety, and (c) do not make a display of yourselves by your appearance, with such things as ornamental jewelry, extravagant hairdos, or extravagant dress.

These exhortations reach the problem area of both sexes. Men have a tendency to be independent, therefore neglecting prayer and becoming skeptical about spiritual things. Since they are typically involved with business dealings, their hands can become a little sticky with unholy things, figuratively speaking, and by nature they have a tendency to be wrathful if opposed or denied.

By the same token, women have a tendency to vanity, especially in their appearance, and this impulse must be controlled. Too, a woman is out of place if she is forward or brazen; she must learn to assume the God-given position that is hers.

Actually, the apostle simply appealed to the better judgment of each sex to steer a moderate course, both inwardly and outwardly, and to avoid extremes. The failure to do so is the cause of much trouble, breeding much confusion in the home, church, and society.

Other passages of Scripture that teach the same principles are Isaiah 3:16-24; Jeremiah 4:30; Ezekiel 23:40-44; and I Peter 3:1-5. Some of them also cite the wearing of makeup as an example of immodesty and ornamentation.

Another admonition regarding modest and appropriate dress is found in Deuteronomy 22:5, which teaches that the distinction between male and female in outward attire is very important to God. "The woman shall not wear that which pertaineth unto a man, neither shall a man put on a woman's garment: for all that do so are abomination unto the LORD thy God."

Fashions, in both men and women's apparel, fluctuate from one extreme to another. The wise convert will soon learn to follow the in-between course as safest.

Some time ago, a denominational church member was dining in St. Louis not far from our World Evangelism Center. Across from the booth where she and her husband were sitting were two young ladies. Unaware that they were the objects of scrutiny, they acted and looked the part of Pentecostals. As the lady later related to a Pentecostal friend, she told her husband, "Those are Pentecostal girls. You can tell by the way they look and act." What a testimony! The lady was impressed by both girls and immediately identified them with the actions and appearance of her Pentecostal acquaintance. We should always appear in public so that any Christian would never need be ashamed of us!

7. Politics

Should a Christian become involved in the political world? When we read the Old Testament, we find many leading characters who were involved in the political world of that time. Many of them were statesmen, and not a few were kings and governors. David, Solomon, and Hezekiah were kings. Nehemiah was a cupbearer for a king, and Joseph was a governor.

In the New Testament, however, we do not find such examples. Instead of Christians being leaders in society, Paul said they were the offscouring of the world (I Corinthians 4:13). He told the Corinthians, "For ye see your calling, brethren, how that not many wise men after the flesh, not many mighty, not many noble are called" (I Corinthians 1:26).

It certainly would be a welcome relief to have government offices manned by genuine Christians. The wheeling and dealing would soon cease. Honesty and virtue would replace corrupt practices. Very few people can, however, stand the tremendous pressure to compromise their Christian testimony by the questionable activities typically associated with political office. If they can, they need to be there!

In any case, every Christian should be a good citizen of the country where they reside. They should not allow their testimony to be hindered by an unconcern for law and order, education, justice, and social needs.

Our Debt to Society

The moment one becomes a member of the church, he becomes indebted. He owes something to every living person! Paul declared that he was in debt to everyone, regardless of his social status. Rich or poor, wise or unwise, civilized or barbarian, everyone has a right to hear the gospel.

We pay that debt by several means. Some may be called to preach, others to be missionaries. Still others will be used of God mightily in personal work. But all of us can labor in prayer, fasting, and sacrificial giving so that others might fulfill their calling.

Each of us must be involved to the limit of the gift that God bestowed upon us! We can do no less. We are all part of a great building, established upon the foundation of the apostles and prophets, with Jesus Christ Himself being the chief cornerstone (Ephesians 2:20). Each of us has a particular part, a given ability, a certain strength, so that when we are effectively united and participate as planned by God, the whole structure of the church grows and extends itself into the world of the unsaved and unreached (Ephesians 4:16).

It should be the earnest endeavor of every born-again New Testament Christian to seek the Lord diligently for divine direction, to find the will of God for his life, and to pursue His will with spiritual determination and enthusiasm, knowing that his contribution to the church, though it may be small, is vital to its overall growth.

Many other things could be written relative to the new Christian's relationship to the world. Your pastor will touch on these things often; thus it is important to be in services at your home church every time possible. You need the church to survive the onslaughts of Satan and to build yourself up in God. Be in church every service, and when it is necessary that you miss, be sure you were not looking for a convenient excuse.

CHAPTER 6

Your Home and You

It has been said, "The light that shines farthest, shines brightest at home." The home has always been recognized as the foundation of our way of life. Examine the success of the country. You will find that it has been derived from the strength of the home.

The home has initiated almost every way of life. Industry and economics were all part of the home in the beginning. For many years the home was a unit of love and relationship with one another. However, the trend over the years has changed drastically, bringing about a disintegration of the family unit.

As a new Christian, you need to understand the importance of the family in nurturing your experience. Understanding Christ as the head of the home will be most important for you.

History indicates that in virtually every great nation or empire there has been a strong family unit. One of the prime factors in the fall of the once great Roman empire was the disintegration of the family. The divorce rate increased greatly in Rome before its fall. In our day we see that lifestyles and home life have been shaken to the roots. Home life today does not compare with that of yesteryear. The loss of love and the lack of strength of parenthood has shattered the modern home. Almost all of the existing problems of our society (such as divorce, crime, child abuse, juvenile delinquency, and drug addiction) can be traced to a failure in the home life.

A look into the Scripture reveals much concerning God's attitude toward the family unit. Paul spoke about home life and its relationship to the church. God has always emphasized the importance of the family relationship. God established companionship and the rearing of children in the beginning.

The home must be a spiritual unit and a foundation for our daily walk with God. Our home life will affect almost everything we do or expect to do in the future, whether it be employment, schooling, or travel. The basic values that we hold are initiated in the home environment.

Relationship between Husband and Wife

The relationship between husband and wife is extremely important in our consideration of the home. Paul gave clear teaching on this matter in Ephesians 5. He told wives to submit to the leadership of their own husbands, and he told husbands to love their wives sacrificially.

Paul likened the relationship between husband and wife to the relationship of Christ with His church. This comparison shows how important the husband-wife relationship really is.

The apostle stated, "Husbands, love your wives, even as Christ also loved the church, and gave himself for it" (Ephesians 5:25). If men loved their wives as much as they love themselves and as much as Christ loves the church, we would see a dramatic change in our homes and in our society.

Concerning the wife Paul wrote, "Therefore as the church is subject unto Christ, so let the wives be to their own husbands in everything." Imagine the change in our homes if every wife respected the husband as the church should respect Christ!

However diligently husbands and wives may try to avoid it, some degree of conflict or misunderstanding will arise sooner or later. It usually results from a breakdown in communication.

When this happens, approach the problem prayerfully with an open mind. Most differences can be settled by a straightforward, loving dialogue between husband and wife. If the matter is not quickly resolved in this way, consult your pastor. While every family spat need not be laid on his doorstep, no situation of potential danger to a marriage should be allowed to develop.

Marital difficulties may be inevitable, but we should always approach them in a mature, adult, and Christian manner. Only when we assume a juvenile attitude do deep problems threaten a marriage relationship.

The adjustment and stability of the child is a reflection of the relationship between husband and wife. If husband and wife provide harmony in the home, most likely the children will be happy and well adjusted. Likewise, if the marital relationship is weak, the child is more apt to be maladjusted. By setting a pattern of love, understanding and affection in the home, we establish a healthy relationship for our children.

Let us suppose that one parent is unsaved. The Scripture does not leave us without instruction concerning this very common situation. I Corinthians 7:14 states: "For the unbelieving husband is sanctified by the wife, and the unbelieving wife is sanctified by the husband: else were your children unclean; but now are they holy." This portion of Scripture lets us know that if we follow the pattern set down in Ephesians 5, we can gradually win our unsaved companion, and our children will be sanctified by our prayers and conduct at home. Our lifestyle and conduct in the home is more important than anywhere else, for what we are at home reflects everywhere else.

Don't try to live a dual standard—one thing at home and another elsewhere. Establish spiritual relationships at home, and you will undoubtedly be spiritual and thoughtful concerning the whole program of the kingdom of God.

Family Altar

The family altar is not a physical altar that has been constructed with hands. The family altar is the relationship a family has with God in their own home.

It is imperative that you have a time of prayer and Scripture reading with your family. Together, offer praise to the Lord and take your problems to Him. Many situations cannot wait until you get to church. It is up to you to show the importance of prayer and Bible reading in your home. Your children should know that God is always available to them.

Make prayer and reading the Scripture a pleasant experience. This will take a little forethought on your part. Do not expect your small children to sit attentively while you read a long passage from the Bible. The length of prayer and of reading is not the most important factor in the family altar.

The time of the day chosen for family altar will not be the same for everyone. It is important, however, for you to establish some time that is convenient for your situation. The presence of a family altar is a must. Do not put off seeking God with your children or your companion. When a problem arises—whether it be in a household purchase, a decision to move, or a change of jobs—pray about it. Look into the Word. God will give direction.

In disciplining your children, you will need the Lord's direction. God has the answer, whatever your dilemma. Remember, your walk with God in full view of family and friends says much about your personal relationship with Him.

Home Environment

Our environment has a profound effect upon us. We would not want to live in a hog pen or lie in the mud. A diet of corn and husks would not be to our liking. Living in a barn among the cows and sheep would prove quite unsatisfactory indeed. It would be an unnatural and uncomfortable environment.

Likewise, the environment of a Christian home cannot be minimized. If Christ is to be the head of your home, you must rid your home of everything that displeases Him.

We must destroy magazines, books, videos, CDs, and Internet links that condone immorality, exploit sex, display nudity, and portray false love. The apostle John wrote, "Love not the world, neither the things that are in the world. If any man love the world, the love of the Father is not in him" (I John 2:15). A relationship with Christ brings about a new environment. Paul declared, "Therefore if any man be in Christ, he is a new creature: old things are passed away; behold all things are become new" (II Corinthians 5:17). When we read worldly literature, it becomes part of us and affects our relationship with Christ. Ultimately it will destroy us spiritually.

Make an effort to cleanse yourself from all that is unlike Christ. God will bless you for it.

A great detriment to our society has been television. The United Pentecostal Church has always stood firmly against the evils of immorality, violence and worldliness that this medium channels into homes. Here again, what we see becomes part of us. Television and movies form a team of destructive forces that rob one of spiritual victory and threatens his life in God. Consequently, the Articles of Faith of the United Pentecostal Church International states, "We wholeheartedly disapprove of our people indulging in any activities which are not conducive to good Christianity and godly living, such as theaters, dances, mixed bathing or swimming, women cutting their hair, makeup, any apparel that immodestly exposes the body, all worldly sports and amusements, and unwholesome radio programs and music. Furthermore, because of the display of all these evils on television, we disapprove of any of our people having television sets in their homes. We admonish all of our people to refrain from any of these practices in the interest of spiritual progress and the soon coming of the Lord for His church."

A good test for the spiritual quality of your home is

this: Would you be comfortable to have Jesus walk into it? The Bible repeatedly says that Jesus is coming again to take His church to heaven. Jesus said His coming would be as a thief in the night. When He comes, there will be no time to rid yourself of worldliness. Determine now that you will be ready for His soon and sudden appearance.